ARIZONA

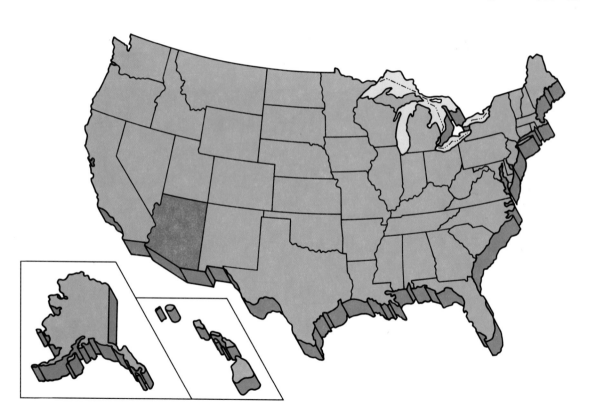

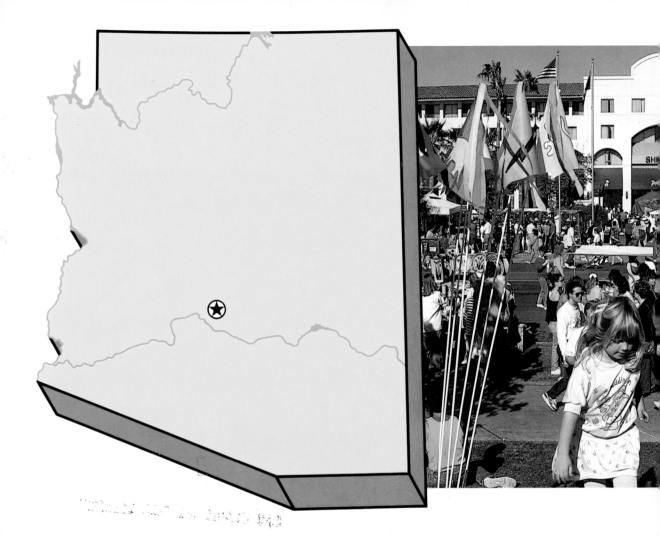

ARIZONA

Dan Filbin

GREAT SEAL OF THE STATE OF ARIZONA · 1912 · DITAT DEUS

Lerner Publications Company

LIBRARY OF CONGRESS
CATALOGING-IN-PUBLICATION DATA
Filbin, Dan.
    Arizona / Dan Filbin.
        p.   cm. — (Hello USA)
    Includes index.
    Summary: Introduces the geography, history, industries, people, and other highlights of Arizona.
    ISBN 0-8225-2705-7 (lib. bdg.)
    1. Arizona—Juvenile literature.
[1. Arizona.] I. Title. II. Series.
F811.3.F55   1991
979.1—dc20   90-38214
                               CIP
                               AC

Cover photographs by Harriet Vander Meer (left) and Jerg Kroener (right).

The glossary that begins on page 68 gives definitions of words shown in **bold type** in the text.

CONTENTS

Did You Know . . . ?

❑ Some of the rock in the deepest parts of Arizona's Grand Canyon are almost 2 billion years old.

❑ People have lived at Oraibi, Arizona, longer than at any other site in the United States. Hopi Indians and their Anasazi ancestors have lived at Oraibi for more than 800 years.

☐ The name *Arizona* comes from an ancient Papago Indian word, *arizonac*, which probably means "small springs." No one knows for sure whether this meaning is exact because members of the Papago tribe no longer use the word.

☐ About 50,000 years ago, a giant meteorite (a chunk of metal or stone from space) struck the earth near the present-day city of Flagstaff, Arizona. The hole the meteorite gouged, known as Meteor Crater, is 570 feet (174 meters) deep and nearly a mile (1.6 kilometers) wide.

This sandstone bluff has a bright, reddish color in the early morning sunshine.

A Trip Around the State

Deserts, forests, mountains, and canyons make Arizona a place full of wonders. Its most famous natural treasure—the Grand Canyon —gives the state its nickname, the Grand Canyon State. Much of this land in the southwestern United States looks as if it has been splashed with rich red, brown, and green paints.

At its northeastern corner, Arizona touches Utah, Colorado, and New Mexico—the only place in the nation where four states meet. Mexico borders Arizona on the south, and California and Nevada lie to the west. The state has three geographic regions—the Northern Plateau, the Central Mountains, and the Southern Desert.

The Northern Plateau, which is really a series of **plateaus** (or flat highlands), makes up two-fifths of Arizona. Over time, winds on the Northern Plateau have sculpted the reddish brown rock into shapes that look like towering needles and huge tabletops. Humphreys Peak, on the southern edge of the plateau region, reaches 12,633 feet (3,832 m) and is the state's highest point.

In the Northern Plateau, the wind has sculpted the land into many amazing shapes.

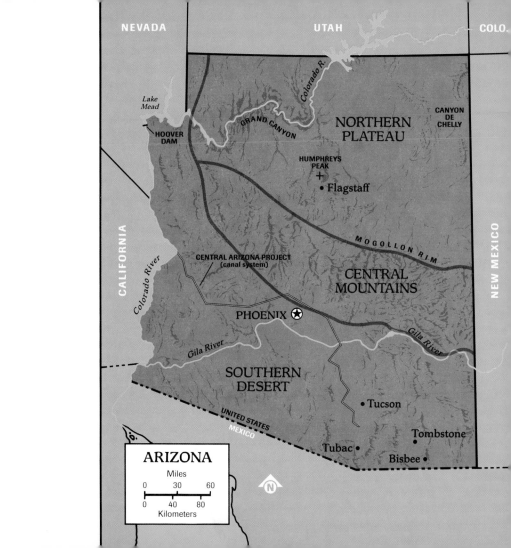

For millions of years, both water from the Colorado River and strong winds have worn down the land, creating the Grand Canyon.

Rivers have cut **canyons** (steep valleys) into the Northern Plateau. The Colorado River began carving the longest and deepest of Arizona's canyons, the Grand Canyon, over a million years ago. The

Deep-green ponderosa pine trees blanket many of the mountains in central Arizona.

valley is 1 mile (1.6 km) deep in some places. As the river cuts still deeper into the valley, the newly exposed layers of rock reveal even more of the earth's history.

The Mogollon Rim—a rock cliff 200 miles (322 km) long—divides the Northern Plateau from the Central Mountains. Millions of years ago, volcanoes and earthquakes formed these mountain peaks.

Forests cast a green hue on the Central Mountains. You may imagine only **deserts** when you think of Arizona, but trees cover one-fifth of the state. In fact, Arizona has the largest stands of ponderosa pine in the United States.

Horseback riders carefully pick their way along a steep mountainside in the southern part of the state.

In the Southern Desert, gently sloping valleys made of rock and sand separate the region's mountain ranges. The desert is dry most of the year. But during the rainy period from July through September, many valleys turn briefly into shallow basins of water. The Southern Desert gets most of its yearly moisture (less than 10 inches, or 25 centimeters) during these three months.

Native to Arizona's Southern Desert, the saguaro cactus is the largest cactus in the United States. The plant can grow to a height of 60 feet (18 m).

Even though the desert gets little rain, some plants grow well there. Mesquite, ironwood, and palo verde trees thrive on the craggy slopes. The long-armed saguaro and the spiny cholla are among the wide variety of cactuses found in the Southern Desert.

Two major rivers flow through Arizona. The Colorado River travels through the northwestern part of the state before cutting south to form most of Arizona's western boundary. The Gila River crosses the southern width of the state and then joins the Colorado River in the southwest.

When the snow melts in Arizona's Central Mountain region, dry streambeds fill with rushing water.

Arizona has a warm and sunny climate. The sun shines on about 8 out of 10 days. Temperatures vary widely in the state because of differences in elevation. On summer days in the Southern Desert, the hottest region, the thermometer often tops 100° F (38° C). But in the Central Mountains, the highest region, temperatures range from 70° to 80° F (21° to 27° C).

In the summer, thunderstorm clouds often bring sudden, hard downpours. Less threatening winter rains occur from December through March throughout much of Arizona. After rains fall, the tangy odor of the creosote bush fills the air in many parts of the state.

Thunderstorms often drench Arizona with short but intense downpours, especially in July and August.

Yucca tree

Prickly pear cactus

Barrel cactus

Roadrunner

18

Gila monster

Mule deer

The Southern Desert's Gila monsters—lizards that are 18 inches (46 cm) long—are the only poisonous lizards in the United States. But they are not as dangerous as one-inch-long (2.5-cm-long) scorpions from the same region.

So many people live in certain areas of Arizona that some animals that once roamed the state have died out. But white-tailed deer and pronghorn antelope still range through the less populated areas.

Arizona's Story

The first people to live in North America came from Asia about 40,000 years ago. Traveling in groups, they crossed over the land that then connected Asia and North America in the northern Pacific Ocean. The descendants of these people are known as Indians, or Native Americans.

For thousands of years, these groups from Asia spread throughout North and South America. Some of the tribes began moving into the region now known as Arizona about 12,000 years ago. At first they hunted herds of large animals for food. Tracking the herds kept them on the move for many months of the year.

More than a thousand years ago, Indians drew people, animals, and plants on rocks in northeastern Arizona.

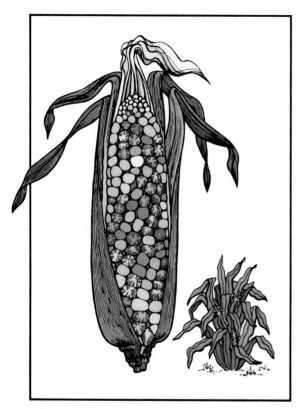

Maize, a type of corn that is easily preserved, made it possible for Indian farmers to store food.

Around 2000 B.C. the Indians learned to grow grains and vegetables from tribes in the area now known as Mexico. Maize, a variety of corn, became a main part of their diet. These farming Indians lived together in permanent settlements and relied on hunting less and less.

Archaeologists have discovered beautifully crafted tools, baskets, and pottery at sites where hunting camps and farming villages once stood. Some of the objects were carved and painted with pictures of animals and human figures that represented spirits.

The Hohokam Indians built irrigation canals about 1,500 years ago.

In the A.D. 500s, an Indian people called the Hohokam built canals to carry water from the Gila River. A form of **irrigation,** this process provided enough water to make maize and other crops grow more easily in the dry climate. About 250 miles (400 km) of canals were constructed, some of which measured 15 feet (4.5 m) deep and 30 feet (9 m) wide. Several of these canals are still used by farmers.

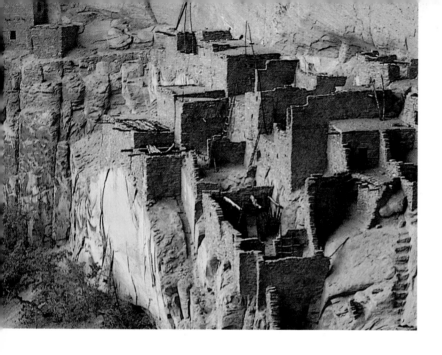

The Betatakin Ruin contains about 135 rooms. The Anasazi began construction on this village around 1250.

By A.D. 800 another tribe, known as the Anasazi, constructed homes that resemble modern apartment buildings. Using stone and mud, these people made square dwellings that were attached to each other. Sometimes the buildings were several stories high, and some were built into the sides of towering cliffs. As many as 1,000 people lived together in some Anasazi communities.

Along a stream in Canyon de Chelly lies the White House Ruin. About 60 rooms are located near the stream and another 10 rooms are built into the face of the huge rock cliff. Constructed in about 1060 by the Anasazi, these buildings probably housed 100 people.

25

Long periods without rain occurred in the late 1200s. The three main groups of Indians in Arizona (the Mogollon, the Hohokam, and the Anasazi) left their large settlements and formed smaller communities. Living in groups of fewer people made it easier for the Indians to grow enough food to feed themselves.

The Hopi Indians are related to the Anasazi group. This drawing shows a Hopi religious ceremony.

This map shows where Arizona's three ancient Indian groups lived in A.D. 1000. Eventually, people from these different groups traded goods with each other and shared farming methods.

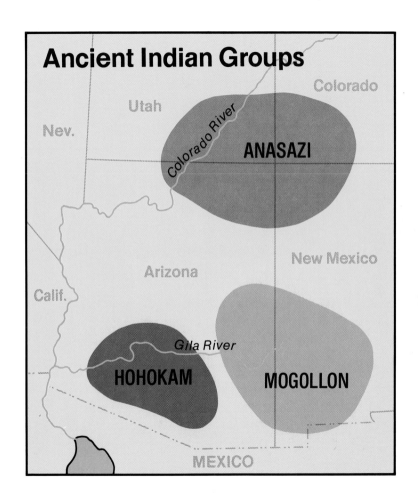

Ancient Indian Groups

Nev.

Utah

Colorado

Colorado River

ANASAZI

Calif.

Arizona

New Mexico

HOHOKAM

Gila River

MOGOLLON

MEXICO

The Apache and the Navajo moved into what is now Arizona probably during the 1200s or 1300s. They came originally from the northwestern part of North America. These Indians specialized in hunting animals. To get food and other supplies, they also raided people who lived nearby.

In the 1500s, Spaniards in search of gold explored the region that would one day become Arizona. Marcos de Niza, a Catholic priest, traveled through the region in 1539, and Francisco Vásquez de Coronado led another expedition the next year. Neither Coronado nor Niza found golden cities. Members of Coronado's group, however, were the first Europeans to discover the Grand Canyon.

Spanish settlers soon followed the earliest Spanish explorers to the region. By 1598 Spaniards had moved to the area, which included Mexico as well as Arizona. Spanish leaders set up a government, making a **colony** called New Spain. Colonial leaders received their instructions from faraway Spain.

In 1692 Eusebio Kino, another Catholic priest sent by the Spanish, built a church that came to be known as San Xavier del Bac. At the villages he visited, Kino worked as a **missionary**, introducing Indians to the Christian religion. He also taught them new ways of raising livestock, fruit trees, and grain. Kino had learned some of these methods from Indians in southern New Spain.

Around 1700, Eusebio Kino and his followers built the church of San Xavier del Bac from clay bricks that had been dried in the sun. In 1783 the church was rebuilt with fire-hardened brick.

The Pima Indians, like their Hohokam ancestors, became skillful farmers.

Not all Indians accepted the missionaries or the Spanish soldiers who came with them. The Spaniards used the Indians as manual laborers to build churches and forts and to grow food. Many Indians did not want to give up their original religion, and they fought to keep the lands that the Spanish wanted to take from them.

At first, Apache and Navajo raiders moved about the territory on foot. But as they captured horses from the Spanish troops, these Indians became even better fighters because they were able to attack and retreat quickly. For protection, the Spanish built forts of **adobe** (bricks of dried clay) at Tubac, Tucson, and other places.

Indian attacks at the end of the 1700s and the beginning of the 1800s drove many Spaniards from settlements in northern New Spain. The Spanish colonial government had less control than before, and Indian leaders saw an opportunity to overthrow Spanish rule. These rebels won independence in 1821, and the lands of Arizona became part of the new nation of Mexico.

HOW TO MAKE ADOBE

1. Sift dirt.

2. Mix sifted dirt with water.

3. Shovel into form and let dry in sun.

4. Remove from form and stack.

In the next 25 years, many U.S. citizens settled in the northern Mexican territory—which included land in what is now Arizona, New Mexico, and California. Border disputes between the United States and Mexico led to war over the boundary between the two countries.

After the Mexican-American War, a **treaty** (peace agreement) signed in 1848 required Mexico to give up some of its territory. According to the agreement, northern Arizona became part of the United States. Then in 1853 the United States bought land from Mexico through the **Gadsden Purchase**. This new piece of U.S. property included the southern part of Arizona.

This territory was far enough south for an east-west postal route to stay open even in winter. Stagecoach drivers and riders on horseback carried the mail across Arizona. Harsh weather made the route difficult for these early postal carriers. Attacks by white outlaws and small groups of Indian raiders were also a constant threat. Mail stations were built along the way to give the postal carriers added protection.

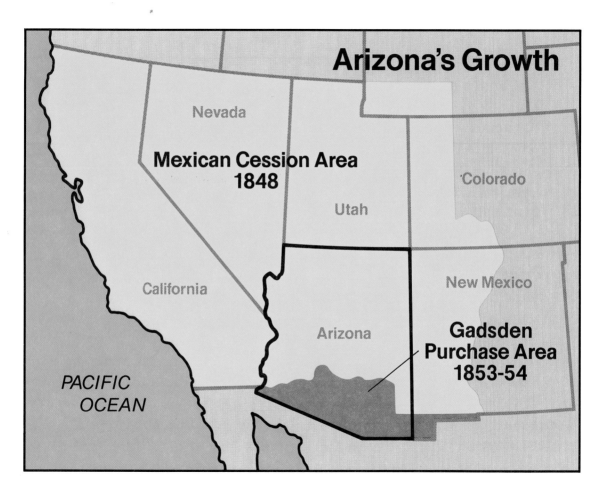

Arizona's Growth

Nevada

Mexican Cession Area
1848

Colorado

Utah

California

New Mexico

Arizona

Gadsden
Purchase Area
1853-54

PACIFIC
OCEAN

Fighting known as the Indian Wars broke out between Indians and U.S. troops from 1860 to 1886. Some Indians went on raids to get food and supplies, but they also fought to keep control of their homelands as more U.S. troops arrived. Kit Carson, an officer in the army, led U.S. soldiers against the Navajo. The army defeated these Indians at Canyon de Chelly in 1864.

Apache fighters continued to raid the residents of Arizona for several years after the Navajo were defeated. Goyathlay (also known as Geronimo), Cochise, and Mangas Coloradas—Apache leaders—launched swift and daring attacks on other Indian tribes as well as on white settlers. By retreating into the rough deserts and mountains, the Apache often avoided capture. But they were greatly outnumbered by U.S. troops.

For many years, the rambling Canyon de Chelly provided a place of safety for Navajo raiders.

While traveling by train to a reservation, Goyathlay *(front row, third from right)* and some members of his Apache tribe are permitted a rest stop.

Goyathlay and his followers surrendered in 1886. Most of the captured Apache warriors and their families were sent to **reservations.** When the Indians arrived at these territories that had been set aside for them, they found that some of the areas were quite unlike their homelands.

A small number of the Apache were sent to Florida or Alabama and later to Oklahoma. But by the end of the 1800s, most Indians from Arizona had been resettled in reservations near their original territories.

During the period of the Indian Wars, a few U.S. **prospectors** found large amounts of silver and copper

Searching for precious minerals was usually slow, backbreaking work for Arizona's prospectors.

in Arizona. These discoveries drew many more people to the region.

New towns grew quickly and were often crowded with residents who had recently made fortunes. Several settlements in Arizona—for example, Tombstone and Bisbee—gained reputations as tough, western towns, where disagreements were sometimes settled by brawls and gunfights.

The number of farmers and ranchers also multiplied during this time. Cowboys tended herds of livestock on Arizona's wide, open land. When the cattle were ready to be sold, cowboys took the animals by means of cattle drives to markets in California or the Midwest. These drives sometimes had herds of 4,000 or more.

In 1912, the year Arizona was admitted to the Union, the first group of state lawmakers met in Phoenix.

By the 1870s, ranchers, prospectors, and others had settled large parts of Arizona, and they began to think about statehood. But it was not until 1912 that the U.S. government accepted Arizona's constitution. The new state was the 48th to join the Union.

The state's first governor, George W. P. Hunt, worked hard to help Arizona's farms and businesses grow. Hunt set aside some of the state's money to build roads and dams. The dams blocked the flow of rivers to collect water for irrigation. Watering their fields through irrigation allowed farmers to till more land. Crops such as cotton became a major part of the state's economy.

During World War II (1939–1945), Arizona's population grew quickly. The state's warm weather and clear flying conditions made it a good place to test airplanes and to train pilots. Airplane manufacturers and military bases moved into the region, drawing many new workers to the state. As the farms and copper mines expanded, more people came to Arizona to pick cotton or dig for valuable minerals.

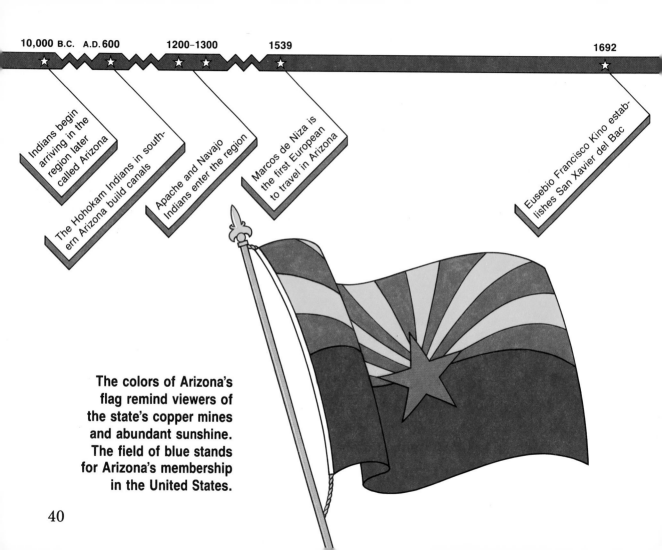

10,000 B.C. **A.D. 600** **1200–1300** **1539** **1692**

Indians begin arriving in the region later called Arizona

The Hohokam Indians in south-ern Arizona build canals

Apache and Navajo Indians enter the region

Marcos de Niza is the first European to travel in Arizona

Eusebio Francisco Kino estab-lishes San Xavier del Bac

The colors of Arizona's
flag remind viewers of
the state's copper mines
and abundant sunshine.
The field of blue stands
for Arizona's membership
in the United States.

40

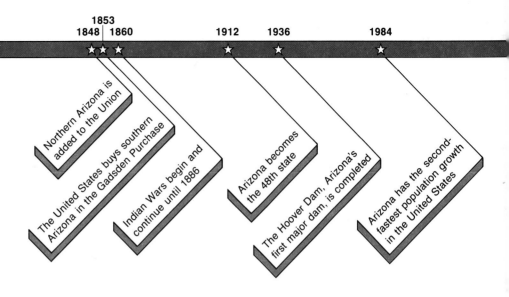

1853					
1848	1860		1912	1936	1984
★	★ ★		★	★	★

Northern Arizona is added to the Union

The United States buys southern Arizona in the Gadsden Purchase

Indian Wars begin and continue until 1886

Arizona becomes the 48th state

The Hoover Dam, Arizona's first major dam, is completed

Arizona has the second-fastest population growth in the United States

Arizona's population continued to grow rapidly after World War II. In the 40 years from 1940 to 1980, the number of Arizonans increased by more than four times. People came from other parts of the United States and from Mexico to work on the farms, in the mines, or in new factories. Many retired people also moved to the state. Arizona remains one of the fastest growing states in the country.

41

Living and Working in Arizona

In the 1800s and early 1900s, people flocked to Arizona to work on the ranches and in the mining towns that sprang up almost overnight. People no longer come to the state in large numbers to work on the land or in the mines, but Arizona's population is still growing fast. One out of seven residents has moved to the state since 1980. By 1990, 3.8 million people were living in Arizona.

A group of Arizonan students *(below)* study geography together. Another young Arizonan *(left)* celebrates his Indian heritage by joining in a ceremonial dance.

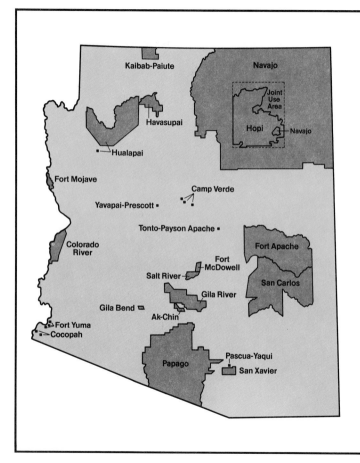

Map labels: Kaibab-Paiute, Navajo, Havasupai, Joint Use Area, Hopi, Navajo, Hualapai, Fort Mojave, Camp Verde, Yavapai-Prescott, Tonto-Payson Apache, Colorado River, Fort Apache, Fort McDowell, Salt River, San Carlos, Gila River, Gila Bend, Ak-Chin, Fort Yuma, Cocopah, Papago, Pascua-Yaqui, San Xavier

INDIAN RESERVATIONS IN ARIZONA

So many immigrants have swelled Arizona's population that the state's original residents—the Indians—make up only about 6 percent of the population. Many Native Americans live on one of the state's 20 reservations.

The largest Indian territory covers more than 13 million acres (more than 5 million hectares) in northeastern Arizona. About 170,000 Navajo live on this reservation. A neighboring tribe —the Hopi—have their own reservation and share the use of some of the Navajo land.

About 16 percent of Arizonans are people of Mexican ancestry. Three percent of the state's residents are black, and 73 percent are white. A small percentage of Arizonans are of Asian ancestry. Most Arizonans live and work in cities and towns, and about half live in Phoenix, the capital city, and its neighboring communities. Tucson, farther to the south, is Arizona's second largest city.

During fiestas (celebrations), dancers enjoy performing in colorful Mexican dress.

Two statues of Navajo people in traditional clothing stand in Phoenix's Heard Museum.

Phoenix and Tucson are the state's largest cultural centers. Among the museums in these two cities are some that display the history of the West. Other attractions include the Champlin Fighter Museum, which exhibits combat planes from the two world wars.

Still other museums have collections of artwork gathered from many parts of the world. The most popular exhibits, however, feature the art of Arizonans, especially that of potters influenced by ancient Indian traditions. Several nature museums, such as the Arizona-Sonora Desert Museum near Tucson, show how the region's plants and animals live in the desert climate.

Painted by a Hopi artist, this artwork shows dancers performing the Hopi corn dance. The ceremony is held during the summer months to help the crop grow better and to bring people closer together.

People in dozens of towns throughout Arizona celebrate their past by holding festivals, rodeos, or fairs. Flagstaff hosts the All Indian Pow Wow, and the mining town of Globe puts on the Copper Dust Stampede Rodeo. Tucson recalls yesterday's cowboys and cowgirls and tests the skill of modern cattle hands during the Fiesta de los Vaqueros.

Many Arizonans enjoy attending sports events. The Phoenix Cardinals of the National Football League (NFL) play their home games at Arizona State University's stadium. Arizona also has a National Basketball Association (NBA) team called the Phoenix Suns, and several major league baseball teams hold spring training in the state.

A member of the Phoenix Suns dribbles the basketball down the court during a home game.

Other favorite activities of Arizonans include camping and boating. Lake Mead in the western part of the state and Theodore Roosevelt Lake northeast of Phoenix are two popular spots for fishing. These and other artificial lakes were created when Arizonans built dams on some of their rivers to collect water for irrigation.

During the winter months, the warmth of Arizona's climate attracts millions of tourists, including a large number of retired people. Many visitors make use of the state's golf courses *(facing page).* **And the Grand Canyon** *(left)* **draws more than three million sightseers per year.**

Over half of the people who work in Arizona earn their livelihoods by providing services—for example, by working in restaurants, stores, banks, schools, and police departments. The second largest group of workers holds jobs in factories. Airplane parts, concrete blocks, parts for computers, and printed materials are some of the items that the state's industries produce.

Arizona is the location for many movies that are set in the Wild West *(right)*. The state is also a center for the development of new technology for airplanes *(below)*.

Mining provides still other jobs in the state. Miners dig for copper and silver in southern Arizona. Earnings from these minerals were large for many years, but since the 1980s they provide only about 3 percent of the state's income. Coal and uranium (used in nuclear energy) are mined mostly in the

In many states a plow like this is used to move snow, but in Arizona it gathers sand for use in construction.

north. Some regions of the state have plenty of sand and gravel, which are used to make roads and buildings.

A long growing season and irrigation help Arizona's crops thrive. Most farms are in the southern part of the state. The main crops include cotton, wheat, citrus fruits, pecans, and dates. Arizona's farms produce more cotton per acre than those in any other state. This is partly because they can grow more than one crop in a year.

A rancher on the Northern Plateau herds his goats to another feeding area. In other parts of northern Arizona, beef cattle and sheep are important agricultural products.

The number of jobs in Arizona grew quickly during the early 1980s. By the end of the decade, however, a large number of residents—both new and longtime—had a hard time finding work. Many people continue to come to Arizona, and state leaders are working to develop more opportunities for employment.

Protecting the Environment

Water is Arizona's most precious resource. At one time, the state had enough water to easily supply its people, plants, and animals. As the number of Arizonans increases, the demand for water also grows. Simple activities such as watering the lawn or taking a shower, when done by more and more people, can quickly use up much of the state's valuable supply of water.

Some of the ways people control and use Arizona's water have caused several plants and animals to become extinct, or die out.

Others are threatened, which means they are in danger of becoming extinct. For example, of the 35 kinds of fish that are native to Arizona, 25 of them are threatened because dams or other building projects are destroying or altering the streams in which the fish live.

Even without the environmental changes caused by humans, the plants and animals of Arizona already face the difficulties of a hot, dry environment. To help them survive, these plants and animals have very effective ways of using and storing water.

The Hoover Dam, located on the Colorado River, holds back enough water to form Lake Mead. At its base, the dam is two football fields thick (660 ft / 200 m).

Mesquite trees, for example, grow deep roots to tap sources of water far underground. Many cactuses have long roots too, but they often spread out near the surface of the desert soil. When it rains, the root system is in position to drink in as much moisture as possible. This ability is crucial, since water is necessary for life.

People also need water. But some of the ways people collect and use water harm the environment. Arizonans have pumped out large amounts of **groundwater** (water from underground) to get more water for agriculture and for use in cities. Almost 85 percent of this water is used to grow crops.

When too much water is pumped from underground, the soil can collapse, leaving cracks in the earth.

A canal, part of the Central Arizona Project, carries water across the Southern Desert from the Colorado River.

So much groundwater has been removed that some land is starting to sink. Even if people completely stopped using groundwater, this resource would take thousands of years to refill itself.

Arizonans have recognized for several decades that water is in short supply. In the 1940s, state leaders began planning the Central Arizona Project, a system of dams, pumps, and canals that takes water from the Colorado River to Phoenix and Tucson. Construction on the project began in the 1970s and was nearly complete in 1990.

Although this project brings water to homes, businesses, and farms in southcentral Arizona, it also has drawbacks. Lakes created by the dams have covered large pieces of land, destroying the orignal plant life and the homes of many animals. Canals make artificial barriers that prevent some wildlife from feeding and roaming in their usual territories.

Millions of gallons of water are removed from the Colorado River each day. This lowers the river's total water level—a practice that leaves the land downstream without the water it needs. Moving water from one place to another means that some people will get less water so that others can have more. Plants and animals are also greatly affected by this environmental change.

With many communities expanding and new ones springing up, Arizona's growth has a big impact on the environment. Arizonans are trying to protect their environment and, at the same time, keep the state growing.

To do this, people are thinking of ways to stretch their water supply. For example, farmers are looking for ways to raise crops with less water, and city planners are trying to figure out more ways to recycle water that has already been used in factories and homes. The state's deserts, mountains, and plateaus—and the water that supports the life in them—need to be cared for wisely.

Arizona's Famous People

EXPLORERS

John Charles Frémont (1813–1890) explored large parts of the western United States, including Arizona. He was also a Union general during the Civil War and governor of the Territory of Arizona from 1878 to 1881.

Eusebio Francisco Kino (1645?–1711) explored much of Arizona and served as a Catholic missionary there. He introduced Arizona's Indians to new ways of raising crops and caring for farm animals.

▲ EUSEBIO KINO

LEADERS

Cesar Chavez (born 1927) grew up in Yuma, Arizona. In 1962 he organized a labor union for farmers called the National Farm Workers Association. Chavez has helped improve living conditions and raise wages for migrant farmworkers throughout the southwestern United States.

John C. Greenway (1872–1926) fought in both the Spanish-American War and World War I. He was one of the first people to successfully develop Arizona's copper mines in the early 1900s.

Sandra Day O'Connor (born 1930) has lived in Arizona almost all of her life. After becoming a lawyer, she won election to the Arizona state senate. Later she served as a judge for the Arizona Court of Appeals. In 1981 she was the first woman to be appointed to the Supreme Court of the United States.

▲ CESAR
CHAVEZ

SANDRA DAY
O'CONNOR ▶

Lynda Carter (born 1951) grew up in Phoenix and became an actress and singer. She starred in the television series "Wonder Woman" during the late 1970s.

Linda Ronstadt (born 1946) grew up in Tucson and became a famous singer of rock, pop, country, and Mexican music. She has many best-selling albums and has starred in plays on Broadway.

LINDA RONSTADT ▶

◀ RAUL CASTRO

▲ BARRY GOLDWATER

◀ GEORGE W.P. HUNT

POLITICIANS

Raul H. Castro (born 1916) became the first Mexican-American governor of Arizona. He was elected in 1974. Castro also has served as a U.S. official in several Central and South American countries.

Barry M. Goldwater (born 1909) is a native of Phoenix, where his family owned a business for many years. He served on the city council and later became a U.S. senator. He was elected as a senator five times, serving a total of 30 years. In the 1964 presidential election, Goldwater ran as the candidate of the Republican party but lost to his Democratic opponent, Lyndon B. Johnson.

George W. P. Hunt (1859–1934) was the first governor of the state of Arizona. He won several terms as governor and was popular with many people for supporting the cause of fair wages for workers.

Andrew E. Douglas (1867–1962) worked for many years as an astronomer and public official. He also studied prehistoric life in Arizona and discovered a way to date ruins by measuring the age of the wood that is found at ancient sites.

Clyde William Tombaugh (born 1906) served as an astronomer at the Lowell Observatory near Flagstaff, Arizona. In 1930 he discovered the planet Pluto by examining a series of photographs taken through the observatory's telescope.

▲ CLYDE WILLIAM TOMBAUGH

▲ GOYATHLAY

SOLDIERS & WARRIORS

William Croft Barnes (1853–1936) was awarded the Congressional Medal of Honor in 1881 for his courage as a scout during battles against the Apache.

Cochise (1812?–1874) was an Apache chief who led his warriors in successful battles against settlers and U.S. troops in Arizona. For more than 10 years, he and his followers used their knowledge of the mountains to avoid the soldiers who were pursuing them.

George Crook (1829–1890) led the U.S. Army in Arizona during its conflicts with the Apache in the 1870s and 1880s. Crook tried to convince the government to settle Arizona's Indians on reservations near their home territory.

Goyathlay (1829–1909), renamed Geronimo by Spanish settlers, was an Apache leader and skillful warrior. He led swift attacks on settlers and soldiers and retreated quickly into Arizona's deserts and rugged mountains. He and his band surrendered to army troops in 1886.

WRITERS

Byrd Baylor (born 1924) grew up on ranches and in mining towns in Texas and Arizona. A resident of Tucson, she writes books for children that explore the natural beauty of the southwest. Some of her books tell about the life and culture of the region's Native Americans. Baylor has won several honors for her work, including prizes for *The Desert Is Theirs* and *The Way to Start a Day.*

◄ BYRD
BAYLOR

◄ ZANE
GREY

ERMA BOMBECK ▶

Erma Bombeck (born 1927) writes a funny newspaper column about the trials of family life. Bombeck began her weekly column in 1963. She has also written several best-selling books, including *I Want to Grow Hair, I Want to Grow Up, I Want to Go to Boise*—a book about children who have survived cancer. She and her family moved to Arizona in 1971.

Zane Grey (1875–1939) wrote novels about the Wild West. He visited Arizona often and lived for a time in Oak Creek Canyon, drawing many of the details of his books from Arizona's landscape. Some of his titles are *Riders of the Purple Sage, The Lone Star Ranger,* and *Call of the Canyon.*

N. Scott Momaday (born 1934) moved with his family to Arizona when he was very young. With a heritage that is part Kiowa and part Cherokee Indian, Momaday often writes about the lives of Native Americans. In 1969 he won a prize for his novel *House Made of Dawn.*

Facts-at-a-Glance

Nickname: Grand Canyon State
Songs: "Arizona," "I Love You Arizona"
Motto: *Ditat Deus* (God Enriches)
Flower: saguaro cactus blossom
Tree: paloverde
Bird: cactus wren

Population: 3,752,000 (1990 estimate)
Rank in population among the states: 23rd
Area: 114,000 sq m (295,260 sq km)
Rank in area, nationwide: 6th
Date and ranking of statehood:
  February 14, 1912, the 48th state
Capital: Phoenix
Major cities (and populations*):
  Phoenix (894,070), Tucson (358,850), Mesa
  (251,430), Tempe (136,480), Glendale (125,820),
  Scottsdale (111,140)
U.S senators: 2
U.S. representatives: 5
Electoral votes: 7

*1986 estimates

Places to visit: Grand Canyon, Petrified Forest in northeastern Arizona, Hopi Indian villages in Navajo County, Arizona-Sonora Desert Museum west of Tucson, Tombstone

Annual events: Cactus Show at Desert Botanical Garden in Phoenix (Feb.), *Cinco de Mayo* (May), White Mountain All-Indian Pow Wow (June), Old Fashioned Mining Camp Celebration in Bisbee (July), Frontier Days in Prescott (July)

Natural resources: copper, sand and gravel, gold, petroleum, pumice, silver, stone, uranium, coal

Agricultural products: beef cattle, cotton and cotton seed, hay, lettuce, wheat, citrus fruits, pecans, dates

Manufactured goods: machinery, electrical equipment, transportation equipment, primary metals, metal products, printed materials, food products, lumber

ENDANGERED SPECIES

Mammals—Sanborn's long-nosed bat, jaguar, Mt. Graham red squirrel, Hualapai Mexican vole

Birds—masked bobwhite (quail), Audubon's crested caracara, thick-billed parrot, wood stork

Reptiles—desert tortoise

Fish—Yaqui catfish, bonytail chub, loach minnow, desert pupfish, Little Colorado spinedace, Colorado squawfish, Gila topminnow, Apache trout

Plants—Arizona agave, Cochise pincushion cactus, Arizona hedgehog cactus, Tumamoc globeberry, Navajo Sedge, Arizona cliff rose

WHERE ARIZONANS WORK

Services—59 percent
(services includes jobs in trade; community, social, & personal services; finance, insurance, & real estate; transportation, communication, & utilities)

Manufacturing—16 percent

Government—13 percent

Construction—8 percent

Mining—3 percent

Agriculture—1 percent

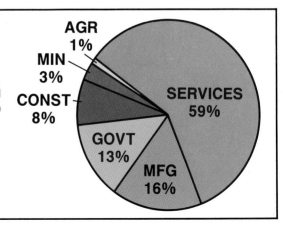

Glossary

adobe   Brick made of clay dried in the sun. The clay is found in Mexico and dry parts of the southwestern United States.

archaeologist   A person who studies ancient times and peoples by digging up what is left of their cities, buildings, tombs, and other remains.

canyon   A narrow valley that has steep, rocky cliffs on its sides.

colony   A territory ruled by a country some distance away.

desert   An area of land that receives only about 10 inches (25 cm) or less of rain or snow a year. Some deserts are mountainous; others are expanses of rock, sand, or salt flats.

Gadsden Purchase A deal in which James Gadsden arranged for the United States to buy land from Mexico in 1853. The United Sates paid $10 million for 29,640 square miles (76,770 sq km) of land south of the Gila River in what is now Arizona and New Mexico.

groundwater Water that lies beneath the earth's surface. The water comes from rain and snow that seeps through soil into the cracks and other openings in rocks. Groundwater supplies wells and springs.

irrigation Watering land by directing water through canals, ditches, pipes, or sprinklers.

missionary A person sent out by a religious group to spread its beliefs to other people.

plateau A large, relatively flat area that stands above the surrounding land.

prospector A person who searches an area for deposits of valuable minerals.

reservation Public land set aside by the government to be used by Native Americans.

treaty An agreement between two or more groups, usually having to do with peace or trade.

69

Index

The photographs and illustrations in this book are used courtesy of:

L.K. Colin, pp. 2–3, 15, 18 (lower right), 48, 52 (both), 55; James Payne, Tonto National Forest, p. 6; Jack Lindstrom, p. 7; Minneapolis Public Library and Information Center, pp. 8, 23, 53; Thomas Henion, pp. 10, 17, 18 (upper left), 19 (left), 20–21, 24, 50, 54, 57; Laura Westlund, pp. 11, 22, 27, 31, 33, 40, 44; Harriet Vander Meer, pp. 12, 13, 19 (right), 71; Sheraton El Conquistador Resort, pp. 14, 45, 51 (both); Ken Palmrose, USDA Forest Service, pp. 16, 60, 69; Jerg Kroener, p. 18 (upper middle); S. A. Johnson, pp. 18 (upper right), 29 (both), 46; © 1990, Sallie G. Sprague, pp. 25, 34–35, 61; Smithsonian Institution, pp. 26, 36; Rhode Island School of Design Museum of Art, p. 30; Arizona Office of Tourism, p. 37; Arizona Historical Society Museum, pp. 38, 62 (upper right), 63 (lower left), 64 (left), 65 (lower left); Phoenix and Valley of the Sun Convention and Visitors Bureau, pp. 42, 43 (left); Rock Leonard, Mesa Public Schools, p. 43 (right); The Museum of Fine Arts, Houston, Gift of Miss Ima Hogg, p. 47; The Phoenix Suns, p. 49; Nebraska Groundwater Foundation, p. 58; Bureau of Reclamation, p. 59; Victor Aleman, p. 62 (lower left); Asman Photo, p. 62 (lower right); James Shea, p. 63 (upper right); Arizona Historical Foundation, p. 63 (upper right); Barry Goldwater, p. 63 (lower right); Lowell Observatory, p. 64 (right); Charles Scribner's Sons, p.65 (right); Rona Kasen, p. 65 (lower right); Jean Matheny, p. 66.